SERGEANT
From the village choir to a Normandy beach: an ATS volunteer's war.

Normandy, June 1944 — "Down! Down! Down!" words that will remain in my mind forever. My heart missed a beat but Army discipline is such (thankfully) that I threw myself down on the ground immediately or my injuries could have been much worse — indeed I might not have survived to tell the tale.

On 3rd September, 1939, when war was declared, eighteen-year-old Elsie Crossley was in Parkwood Chapel — she sang in the choir.

On 6th January, 1946, twenty-five-year old ATS Sergeant Elsie Crossley was demobbed at Fulford Barracks, York — she was still singing.

Elsie's account of her life between those dates, complemented with many photos and documents, etc., will be informative for some, nostalgic for others and a delightful read for all.

SERGEANT

From the village choir to a Normandy beach: an ATS volunteer's war.

Elsie M. Crossley

ARTHUR H. STOCKWELL LTD.
Torrs Park   Ilfracombe   Devon
Established 1898
www.ahstockwell.co.uk

British Library Cataloguing-in-Publication Data.
A catalogue record for this book is available
from the British Library.

This book is dedicated to all the ATS girls I ever knew.

My thanks to Jackie and David for the initial typing of my manuscript.

To Ted Brandrick for his care in reproducing many of the photographs.

To my dear Ray for his valuable advice in the extension of my manuscript, the consequential re-typing, his continuous support without which I might have given up, and without whom I would not have completed the story.

ISBN 0 7223 3646-2
Printed in Great Britain by
Arthur H. Stockwell Ltd.
Torrs Park   Ilfracombe
Devon

CONTENTS

CHAPTER 1

Sunday, 3rd September 1939

I wakened at about 8 o'clock with a sense of foreboding. I made my way to the bathroom and got dressed — then wakened my two young sisters. I was always up first on Sunday mornings and had to get breakfast for myself (I was eighteen years old) and my two sisters. I chivvied them along to get washed and dressed and gave them breakfast — then got them off to Sunday school.

After washing-up I dressed in my 'Sunday Best' ready to go across the fields to sing in the choir at Parkwood Chapel. On my way out of the garden gate I 'nicked' one of my dad's pansies for my buttonhole. Dad and I both pretended he did not know — but I think he counted them.

I arrived, as usual, about three minutes before 10.30 to be greeted by Dorothy Lizzie, (i/c choir), "Come on Elsie — you've just made it."

But it was a very sombre choir that filed up into chapel to the choir seats that morning. Our beloved pastor, Rev Fred Smith, led the way and all stood silent in church — waiting for him to speak.

"I am going to return to the manse," — he said "and listen to the radio (wireless in those days), for the 11 o'clock announcement. Will you please all say a prayer and sing hymns until I return?" It was at that time, unheard of to bring a wireless into church.

We knew what was to come and the older ones shed a few tears but I think most of us young ones felt a tremor of

7

— excitement — perhaps — of the unknown.

At 11.15 dear Rev Smith returned — white faced — to us and spoke from the pulpit. "I have, with sorrow, to tell you that we are now at war with Germany." After another prayer (not that we were all concentrating), he dispersed us to our homes.

The next day being Monday everyone available was rushing around the shops in town (Huddersfield), three miles away, trying to buy blackout material to put up at the windows. We had been *'ordered'* to do this so that no chink of light would show to enemy aircraft. Groups of wardens were gathered locally to patrol and inspect at night and often was the cry heard, "Put that light out!"

Within three days we had an air-raid warning — that horrible wailing sound which carried up the valley. It put the fear of death into us — as these sirens were all fixed to the mill chimneys, and sounded most eerie.

My father cut out a wall into the cavity below our sitting room to use as an air-raid shelter. All was activity and everyone was involved in some kind of preparation. The mills all turned to making khaki cloth for Army uniforms and Air Force blue for the RAF.

Young men began to be 'called up' for service and training in the Forces. Starting with the nineteen year olds to twenty year men (boys!). It was not long before the youngest of my brothers — Frank — received his 'calling up papers' and quit his job to be placed in the Royal Artillery. He eventually became a driver of Army lorries.

We had a number of air raids and 'warnings' at about this time and some bigger raids took place over Manchester — we could at times see the glow from fires in the sky from both Manchester and Leeds.

About four months later my next brother Harold (a painter and decorator of some merit and much liked locally) was also called up into the Royal Engineers. My mother was devastated; two out of three of her beloved boys.

Shortly after all this the following late Spring brought 'Dunkirk' and our chapel Sunday school was commandeered to take in a number of these shocked young soldiers. Everything was changed.

At Parkwood Chapel, which was the centre of our social life, I taught the infants at afternoon Sunday school. I sang in the choir for five years and occasionally was given a Sunday anthem solo. I took part in everything that I could — plays, Gilbert and Sullivan and singing solos at many functions. At one, never to be forgotten, Rev Fred Smith gave a talk on "The Stars". I followed this quite innocently with my solo 'Not understood'. I never lived it down. I used to play the piano for hymns — especially at our youth Bible class, where 'Onward Christian Soldiers' was a great favourite — especially with the 'lads'. They used to raise the roof. It was all happy and enjoyable — with few free evenings and good friendships, walks on Sunday evenings and tea at our various houses.

When I went into the ATS Fred Smith presented me with his own inscribed hymn book 'for services to Parkwood'. I still have it after sixty years. It is a bit battered as it has been well used — but well loved.

Myself and similar aged friends — boys and girls from Parkwood, decided to have one good day out together. Innocent as we were in those days — a ramble over the moors and a packet of sandwiches with us — dare we call at that 'pub' and have a shandy? The minister's daughter was with us but she fell in with the plans and did not 'shop us'.

Little did we know that that was the very last time our 'gang' would ever be together. All the boys, bar one, went into various services — two did not return, killed in action — one in the Navy, 'little Jack' and one in the RAF, Elwyn, a clever musician and one went to Canada. Of us girls — two went into the Land Army, one into the WAAF and two of us into the ATS. I have photos of that last day together. Treasured.

During this waiting period of 'Cold War', Norman, my eldest brother, made friends with a Welsh soldier stationed with the Royal Signals in Huddersfield and brought him home to have tea with us. Eventually Bob and I (James Robert Jones) fell in love and we became engaged. Bob was

9

A happy group from Parkwood Chapel (1940).
Elsie third from left; Kathleen (see page 35) second from right.

posted overseas to the Far East and after one or two letters
I heard no more. Some time later his mother wrote to say
that he was 'missing, presumed prisoner of the Japanese'.

Quite recently a friend of mine (an officer in the Royal
British Legion) made enquiries on my behalf of The
Commonwealth War Graves Commission to establish what
had happened to Bob (James Robert Jones, Signalman). It
transpired that Bob had died on the 2nd December 1942 at
the hands of the Japanese whilst a POW. I now have the
relevant documents of this. A brave young man.

My eldest brother, Norman, was a plumber by trade and
was exempt from the services. This disgusted him and he
tried again and again to join the Royal Navy. He had always
loved the sea. He was turned down and was very upset
about this. To make matters worse he was directed to the
Glasgow shipyards to work on ships requiring plumbing
work whilst in dock.

My three brothers were now away and an idea was

forming in my mind. I asked my parents if I could join the services but my dad said "No! When you are twenty-one you can do as you like, but until then you stay at home. There are enough away from this house." That was the rule in those days.

At this time I was learning the trade of inspecting for faults in Worstead (in Yorkshire — Werstead, not Worstead) material — extremely fine cloth for suitings and officers' uniforms made at Longwood Finishing Co. (just across the fields from my home).

I was a smart, well dressed and possibly attractive girl and it became noticeable to others that the young manager and designer, Ron, visited my desk table more frequently than the others! He asked me out to a dinner dance at a fine hotel in Halifax (he was one of the few who owned a car!) and there I met his mother and sister. He was nice company.

Shortly afterwards he did ask me to marry him — but knowing that I wanted to join the ATS I am afraid I put him off for a time. (I probably made a mistake there, as he was regarded as a good 'catch'. I do not mean that derisively — he really was nice and actually he was very kind and attentive.) More of him later. Maybe I should have said "Yes".

I have always had a mind of my own and went to work secretly in the following weeks. Visiting enrolment offices in Huddersfield I found that, at that time, when I was nineteen, I could enlist *without* my parents' consent.

I did just that. Went for a medical and, of course, being a tough Yorkshire girl — I passed OK.

Ten days later, in Spring 1941, a letter arrived at our house calling me up for service as a *volunteer* (this was important to me) into the ATS to report to Fulford Barracks at York. I then showed the letter to my parents and all hell broke loose. The rest follows.

AUXILIARY TERRITORIAL SERVICE

CONDITIONS OF SERVICE AND APPLICATION FORM

PART I. General Conditions.

The General Conditions of your Enrolment are as follows :—

1.—To serve as a member of the A.T.S. for the period of the present emergency so long as your services are required.

2.—To perform full time service at any locality at home or overseas, as may be required.

3.—To obey all orders given by your superiors.

4.—To remain a member of the A.T.S. until duly discharged. The usual grounds for discharge are :—

    (a) Termination of period of enrolment.

    (b) Compassionate grounds.

    (c) Medical grounds.

    (d) Service no longer required.

PART II. General Information.

1.—Members of the A.T.S. replace soldiers in certain selected duties, including :—

    (a) Clerks (shorthand writers, typists, pay clerks) ;

    (b) Cooks (for Officers', Sergeants' and Men's messes) ;

    (c) Drivers I.C. (ambulances, cars, light vans, etc.) ;

    (d) Orderlies (mess orderlies, messengers, telephone orderlies, etc.) ;

    (e) Storewomen (equipment, clothing, P.A.D. stores, etc. : clerical qualifications are needed for book-keeping in stores) ;

    (f) Specialists (Teleprinter and telephone switchboard operators : kine theodolite operators—photographic training needed).

Conditions of service.

Army Form E 511 R

AUXILIARY TERRITORIAL SERVICE
NOTICE TO REPORT FOR DUTY

Date ___8th_____, 1941.   Recruiting Office,

~~Mrs E M Crosley.~~   ___HUDDERSFIELD.___

      I have to inform you that you are now required to report for duty in the Auxiliary Territorial Service.

      I am therefore to request that you will report to the Officer Commanding No. 2 A.T.S. Training Centre, York, on __17th_____, 1941,____ A railway ~~bus~~ warrant for your journey is enclosed herewith.

      You should report as early in the day as possible.

Leave Huddersfield 9am
Arrive York 11-38am.

                                           Captain,
Re~~Recruiting Officer~~,
Centre No. 76, HUDDERSFIELD.

WT. 42041/414 50,000 1/40 KJL/40 Gp. 698/3 Forms E 511 R
WT. 11121/225 100M 5/41 KJL/5228/3 Gp. 698/3

Report for duty.

CLOTHING. 2 pairs of pyjamas or nightgowns are essential.

    You will be issued with a complete uniform and necessaries on arrival at the Depot, but the following would be useful if you wish to bring them with you:

1 Woollen cardigan.	1 Towel.
1 Tooth brush	1 Sponge or equivalent.
1 Housewife, with buttons, needles and thread.	6 Handkerchiefs.
	1 pair gym. shoes.
1 Complete set of underclothing, including 1 pair knickers.	

GENERAL INSTRUCTIONS

Bring your
  (a) National Registration Book. (b) Ration Book. (c) Civilian Gas Respirator.

If your Health Insurance Contribution Card and/or Unemployment Book are in the possession of your employer or of the Employment Exchange, you should obtain them, if possible, and bring them with you. But IF YOU ARE UNABLE TO GET THEM YOU MUST NOT DELAY JOINING ON THIS ACCOUNT. If you have to apply to the Employment Exchange for your Unemployment Book, you should take with you the Receipt Card (U.I.40) and this notice.

If your Unemployment Book is with the Exchange and you cannot get it, you should bring the Receipt Card with you instead and hand it in on joining.

What to bring.

CHAPTER 2

Fulford Barracks

As if never to return, I was seen off at Huddersfield Station by my parents, two aunts and my sisters. They cried — I did not! It was an exciting new phase in my life and although in the next few years it was sometimes frightening, always hard work, I have never regretted it. What I did regret later that day and the next, was wearing a smart blue tweed suit. Skirts at that time were worn just below the knee and jackets medium hip level (more of that later).

At the next two stops of the train two more prospective ATS joined me and we soon arrived at York Station with our required case with toothbrush etc. There were no family cars in those days and with few visits to local towns and cities this meant that these were almost 'foreign parts' to us.

At the end of the platform stood a large and very smart male sergeant (Sergeant Atha, we soon learned) of the West Yorkshire Regiment, who gathered us together by shouting "ATS this way!"

Along with the others I carried my case to the exit and there, waiting for us, was our transport; a 3-ton Army truck with the back let down for 'easy' access! We all needed a push and pull aboard, my skirt riding up and showing more than was decorous in those days.

We were driven through the streets of York, with the occupants leaning out to see as much as possible, and then out to Fulford Barracks — No. 2 ATS Training Centre which was to be home for some four weeks — and for others like myself for much longer.

We alighted (such a dainty word!), more like tumbled out, outside a barrack block — which transpired to be Ripon Block — No. 3 Company ATS and were taken upstairs to a large room, down the centre of which were single iron beds (and metal wardrobes) placed head to head alternately.

I was given the seventh bed up on the right and found that the ones either side of me already had a case upon them. Such was wartime and the luck of the draw — I found two good friends. On one side was Sally Reid — a little 'Geordie' girl, and on the other side was The Hon Mary Markham — quite a lady and what a good open sport she was. From her weekend leave Mary brought me back from London a lovely black and grey striped blouse which I saved until after the war and wore it gladly. (I do have a photo wearing this on my first holiday for seven years at Butlins, Skegness!)

On the very solid beds were three Army biscuits; quite rightly named — they were as hard as dog biscuits and three rigidly folded dark blankets and a pillow. I became used to the hard mattresses eventually and they did have their use. We found that after folding our skirts carefully and placing them under the mattresses at night, we had a beautifully 'cornered' skirt in the morning!

It was now about midday and we were each 'issued' (you are not 'given' in the Army — you are issued) with a knife, a fork and a dessert size spoon — with strict instructions that we were never, ever, to leave them behind anywhere or dire consequences would follow!

We were called out of our barrack room by the aforesaid Sergeant Atha and led around the barrack square to the mess (cook house). Here we filed in and sat eight to a table and our dinner duly arrived; lovely stew with potatoes and one slice of bread. I was so hungry — it was hours since my breakfast and it really was good. It was followed by a steamed pudding — it was nearly always this or rice pudding — then we were told to stand and file out.

At the door was a bucket of hot water in which we had

to dip our 'eating irons' as they became known, prior to washing them in the ablutions back in our block. The ablutions were within the same block and consisted of a row of about twenty 'loos' and opposite them against the other wall twenty wash basins (hot and cold). You washed completely in the open.

That first afternoon we were given a 'medical' and oh how I longed for a longer coat instead of my little jacket! We had to strip off all except knickers and jacket (or coat!). We were a modest lot at that time and although I came from a large family I had never 'stripped off' in front of anyone before and there we all were — all shapes and sizes — killing ourselves laughing — particularly those like myself with only a short jacket to cover my modesty!

After that we were ushered back to the barrack room to find that all the beds were now taken by girls and women from all over the country (we were amongst the last volunteers — after this mostly they were conscripted) and there were thirty of us and a girl corporal, who had her bed near to the door.

Next we were shown how to make up our bed having been issued with two sheets and a pillowcase.

Tea time came and again over to the cookhouse for tea; bread and jam and a piece of slab cake and a mug of tea (we now had an enamel mug each).

The evening was ours — confined to barracks of course. We did not see the outside world again for two weeks — until we had been completely uniformed and smartened up. There had been much silence through the day — shock perhaps, maybe a bit of homesickness with some (not me!) but now tongues were loosened and we got to know each other. We soon discovered that every evening between 8.00 and 9.00 p.m., if we went over to the cookhouse we could get a cup of cocoa and a piece of cake for supper.

Day began next morning with 'Reveille' at 6.00 a.m. — enough to make anyone shoot out of bed. The Regimental Bugler had his stance right outside my nearest window, which had to be opened at night. So he sounded 'Reveille' every morning, at 6.00 a.m. and 'Lights Out' at 10.30 every night, which meant *lights out*. If you were not ready for bed, you did the rest in darkness.

We were exhorted by our corporal to fold up all our sheets and blankets correctly, get washed and dressed and line up outside for 7.15. This was our first initiation into the perpetual marching in ranks of three, to go *around* the barrack square (never *over* it unless on parade) for breakfast (usually a spoonful of scrambled egg — dried egg! — or one slice of bacon, two slices of bread, marmalade or jam and a mug of tea). Any 'flab' we had was soon lost with this and drill in the next week or two.

The following three or four days were taken up with being issued with uniforms, given a pay book and Army number which you never forgot — mine — W/89104 (I was one of the early ones), and being sworn in to be loyal to the Sovereign — eight at a time.

With our uniform were some undies but no knickers, at that time we had to supply our own! It was not long before we were issued with knickers though; two pairs of white warm ones and two pairs of khaki silk knitted ones. These were the *Directoire* type which we immediately christened 'tank traps', nevertheless they were comfortable and we were glad of them.

We stood before an ATS officer and she said something like, "Six and a half hat, five shirt, six jacket, four skirt, six shoes" and you would be moved quickly down the line to pick up these items which were being handed out smartly by the 'minions'! Being average height and size I was lucky that my clothes (sorry uniform) fitted. I must add that although some were issued with too long skirts, or jackets that perhaps did not meet to 'do up', the Army tailors soon got to work on them and we all looked pretty good on our first parade.

We had kit inspections when everything had to be laid out in proper order on our beds and we stood to attention beside our own bed whilst our officer and CSM inspected. Anything missing we had to pay for.

Our Army pay was just 10/- (now equal to 50p) a week and we learned to parade for this — show our Army pay book in the left hand and salute the officer with our right hand and then collect the precious ten shillings.

We were soon organised into a decent squad to 'fall in' in ranks of three. Taught how to march, turn, salute and hold ourselves well. The male sergeants trained us — some of us later were to take on that job, and the male RSM (Mr Murfitt) supervised, occasionally taking over. He had to be seen to be believed. So smart — we certainly respected him.

I was certainly beginning to 'fit in' and although this kind of training was quite tough, I enjoyed it. We were kept on the go from 6.30 a.m. to 5.00 p.m., and at that time — until we became used to all this movement and exercise we were glad to relax in the barrack room in the evenings, or go along to the NAAFI for a cup of tea and a chat with other girls. If any chocolate had arrived there the news spread like wildfire — we were allowed one bar each (small size) and I used to hoard mine to take home to my young sisters when I had a weekend off. Not that I did not enjoy chocolate but we did have quite good rations in food and my family were struggling on less. (Perhaps this is why I now really do enjoy chocolate!)

During all these two weeks we had a dental inspection and 'jabs' against this, that and the other. Also we had aptitude tests and some written exams to sort us out for when we were given our future training for jobs in the Auxiliary Territorial Service. There were four companies of 120 girls and women in each — I was in No. 3 Coy with a green shoulder flash.

We began to have drill in turn on the barrack square, supervised by RSM Murfitt. He would choose a recruit now and then to demonstrate a particular drill movement. "Private Crossley!" I heard one day shouted across the square.

'Me.' I thought, 'Oh dear!' I came to attention and made my smartish way to his side where I had to demonstrate a salute. All seemed to go well. Oh! At times those poor limping feet in new shoes. My toes have never been quite the same — but I still walk quite smartly and I have never slouched!

The Hon Mary (next bed) used to quite hate the marching. "My dear!" she would say to me, "just wait until I tell my darling Paul about all this!"

The camaraderie was something never to be forgotten and we strove to be the best platoon ever.

At the end of three weeks we were each interviewed by a panel of officers to determine what trade or job we were to follow. I was told that I was suitable to go into Radio Location (plotting incoming aircraft for the ack- ack guns) but I had been chosen as Chief Recruit for my platoon and that with one from each of the other platoons in all the four companies I was going to be trained as a Training NCO — first a corporal and later if suitable as a sergeant. I could not believe this. I knew I had worked hard but I was very proud of the honour.

AN OLD ENVELOPE
AT THE END OF MY
FIRST month

NOTE THE STAMP.
ONE PENNY (WAS)
ENVELOPE SEALED

W/89104 Ch/Rec. Crossley. E.M.
No 2. A.T.S. Training Centre,
I.T.C. West Yorks. Regt
No. 7 Room, Downe Block.
Holding Coy.,
Fulford Barracks
York.

Envelope to 'Chief Recruit'.

At the end of our training (four weeks) I was detailed to get together any 'talent' in the company and put on an end of training concert. Having helped at Parkwood (my chapel) with such things I did this wholeheartedly — and of course took the opportunity of singing a solo or two to keep my voice going.

I should add that I now had a green chevron on my upper sleeve, this to denote Chief Recruit, (much like a lance corporal) and I felt very conspicuous. There was no jealousy amongst my room mates — a fierce friendship and always help from little Sally Reid who stayed on at the barracks to become an orderly.

On the medical side I had to have a tooth removed and was allowed the afternoon 'off duty'. Our CSM (male at that time) came to see if I was OK. He was an old soldier and quite a dear. We secretly called him 'Daddy'.

We shortly after this had an ATS CSM (Wright) who was most helpful. Our company officer was Subaltern — soon to become Junior Commander (Captain) Kay Burnett. She was extremely smart and very good looking and also a good officer. She once burned a cigarette hole in her skirt and knowing I was from the worsted trade asked me if I could do anything about it. I 'invisibly' mended it for her and she asked me to her parents' home for a day. Eventually she married and became Junior Commander Taylor.

As I said before we had to keep our barrack room spotless. Orderly officer for the day — complete with retinue — CSM and sergeant inspected every day. The officer would run her finger over any high ledges to make sure that they had been dusted. Windows had to be cleaned. We learned to do this with 'screwed up' newspaper — the print did the trick complete with elbow grease. (Try it. It does work!)

At the end of four weeks we put on our company concert in the hall where we had lectures. Then we were sent home for thirty-six hour leave. Guess who was waiting to take me out? Ron — who once more asked me to marry him!

Returning to barracks the company was all posted out to their second training as clerks, orderlies, cooks, ack-ack, drivers, signals and numerous other important and useful occupations to release the men for fighting.

As Chief Recruit I stayed on at Fulford Barracks to await the start of a corporal cadre (course). I got on the wrong side of an unhappy lance corporal who was not chosen to go on the cadre and she was given the task of finding us, awaiting the course, jobs around the depot. Along with a London girl from another company she sent us to clean out the men's loos. Along came my little guardian angel Sally Reid "Come with me" she said "I'll help you" and she did just that.

In fact Lance Corporal Freeman, with her ginger hair, had done me quite a good turn, for the girl I was detailed with was also a singer (of pop music — whilst mine was ballads and musical shows stuff) and we became very firm friends. Doreen Pickering was her name and we sang at many concerts together — more later — and shared our parcels from home (and cash!).

We had wonderful church parades with the West Yorkshire Regimental Band and RSM Murfitt leading the way out of the depot, down the road for half a mile to the men's barracks and the church. People all stopped to see us, for the ATS on parade was a new thing and we were very smart.

I had been a private in the Army for three and a half weeks only. Doreen and I used to spend our Saturday afternoons and evenings in York — a city we both loved. Wherever we went we had to carry on our backs our large pack, respirator (about 7 lbs in weight) and our steel helmet *not* tin hat). We felt like pack horses.

The evenings were now 'drawing in' and it was dark by 9.00 p.m. As we had to be in barracks by 10.00 p.m. we usually left the city by about 8.45 p.m. to walk back (about two miles, we could not afford the bus fare!). Our first return was quite a shock. There were soldiers with rifles on duty at the gate.

"HALT! Who goes there?" said one. "Friend or foe?"

"My God!" said Doreen, "say friend or he'll shoot!"

"Friend" I said — wobbly.

"Take one pace forward and be recognised." Which, of

course, we did. With a broad grin on his face the soldier said, "Pass, friend" and in we went.

We looked forward to letters and I started to get the occasional one from my brothers — photographed air mail. I still have some of them from the Middle East war zone.

By this time we had an arrangement with a Chinese laundry in York to launder and starch our shirt collars. We used to save up a couple weeks' collars (all with our names on of course — as the rest of our kit) and in turn do the 'laundry run'. The rest of our laundry was done by the Army — weekly. For example — one of everything was allowed, to a total of seven items!

CHAPTER 3

Promotion

At last enough of us were detailed to begin the corporal cadre. Twelve of us altogether. We now had an ATS RSM (one of the first to hold this rank in the ATS), her name was Miss Elsie May (same as mine) Scarborough. We all loved her and respected her.

Both she and RSM Murfitt instructed us on the course and we were very hard worked. We were segregated from our companies and both our kit and ourselves had to be perfect. Inspection every day.

No matter what the weather was like — drill and learning how to teach it, took place every morning from 9.00 a.m. to 11.00 a.m. I well remember a hailstorm and the RSM stood there with his 'ramrod' back and continued to drill us! Toughening up process! Fortunately by now we had two uniforms. One for daily duty and one for best and main parades — (our No. 1 uniform). Lectures for hours and five mile marches.

The course lasted three weeks and all of us bar one, passed out. We were called to a special parade and one by one our names were called and we had to go forward to the CO to receive our corporal stripes. A proud moment.

It might be of interest to note that no make-up was allowed and hair length had to be off the collar. No exceptions were made.

Two weeks later one Saturday morning I was called to the Company Office. 'Hope I haven't done anything' was

Doreen Pickering.

RSM Scarborough.

my first thought.

I knocked — went in and saluted my officer — Junior Commander Burnett — she said, "At ease, Corporal — look behind you!" Seated behind the door were my mother and father.

'Good grief' I thought 'fancy coming here unannounced.' I was very embarrassed. They had no idea of Army discipline.

Miss Burnett smilingly gave me the day off to go out with them. It transpired that Ron had brought them in his car, which was not allowed in the depot — he was waiting outside with it. We spent a happy day in York.

The following Saturday Doreen and I went out to celebrate our promotion. The London show "Old Chelsea" — starring the famous tenor Richard Tauber — had been bombed out of their London theatre and come up to York. We had saved two weeks' pay and booked for it. We went to 'Betty's' tea house for cakes and tea — then on to the show. Being corporals we were now allowed to stay out until 10.30. A lovely day to remember. I still have my copy of "My Heart and I" — which I sang whilst playing the part of Princess Balroubadour in 'Aladdin' some time later at Normanton Barracks, Derby. More eventually of this.

The new intake of recruits was now due and I was given my own platoon (I still have photos of many of these girls). I worked them hard but with respect on both sides. I cared for the younger ones (two of them only seventeen who had 'got in' on false age giving). Each night at lights out I went around to every bed to see if the occupant was alright.

After three and a half weeks they were ready to 'pass out' and we put on the now usual company concert.

One more intake after this and I was given my first eight days' leave. I again had a date with Ron when I had sadly to make it clear that I was not ready for marriage and had decided to continue with the Army. Actually there was no way out of the Army then except by Para II of King's Regulations (pregnancy!).

I went to chapel at Parkwood on Sunday morning where there was much handshaking and fuss made of me. They

1st Squad. Dec. 1941

M. Schleider.

Winifred Avey.

Dorothy Bigham *The best ...*

Vera Hills

Gladys Stancerk.

Vera M. Hanser.

Doreen Upson (Betty)

Gwen Nichols. Best wishes - Luck (Nick).

Ivy Waterton.

Pat. McMullen. (Best wishes always)

Renée Watkins. (All my love.)

Rose Charles (wishing you all the)
(happiness)
(in the world)

Lilian Compton Yo the Best
Corporal
P. Cockrill. "The Little Mother —

Jean Rutherford (Cheer up Chick!!!)

Celia Brett.

Eva Cooper.

Jenny Deune. To "Mum", who made
our 3 weeks in York to
(Don't forget to be a to you) happier in our lives.
— mama girls)

Nominal roll — the author's first squad as a corporal.

were kind people and used to knit gloves and scarves for us in the forces and made money at 'dos' to send us a small postal order now and again. Much appreciated. I returned to York.

At about this time there was a great shortage of paper in the country and toilet paper was distinctly in short supply. You'll never believe this but it is quite true! I lined up my platoon as was usual for pay parade on a Friday. It was the custom — as NCO in charge to be paid first. March up to the desk. Halt. Salute and to my utter amazement was given my pay in one hand and *seven sheets of toilet paper* in the other. "That I'm afraid" said Junior Commander Burnett, trying not to smile "this is your ration for the week." I cannot now imagine how we managed, but being an inventive sort of person I suppose I found a way (along with my Army photos I still have one of those sheets).

Throughout my service in the ATS Thursday night was 'Barrack Night'. No one was allowed out. You had to clean the room thoroughly and do all your odd jobs of sewing, hair washing, etc., and, hopefully, if not on duty a visit to the NAAFI (in barracks) for a cuppa.

Not all evenings were free. At least one in four was a detailed evening 'fire watch' in the depot until 12.00 midnight, and one day per week was duty NCO for the Company. Sometimes this lasted all night.

There were NAAFI dances and the company concert. I always sang a solo or two and was beginning to be asked to other barracks nearby and Strensall Barracks, York to sing at their 'dos' for the soldiers.

Came December 9th 1941, my twenty-first birthday. I thought no one knew — but the platoon had joined forces and bought me a lovely leather toilet case (it must have been hard to come by). I was up and dressed and at 9.00 a.m. was told to report to Company Office. I knocked on the door (a bit apprehensively) entered and as is usual saluted.

Miss Burnett said, "I understand it is your twenty-first birthday. If I give you a thirty-six hour pass can you get home today and return tomorrow?"

The author's twenty-first birthday card from her squad.

What joy! Who said the Army hadn't a heart?

It was not all joy nevertheless as this was the day (in this country — the 8th December in the USA) of the bombing of Pearl Harbour and the cause of the Americans entering the war. As I write this on the 8th May — a fly-past is actually taking place overhead to celebrate V-E Day (Victory in Europe), 1945.

Back to my twenty-first. After rides in three buses — York to Leeds — Leeds to Huddersfield — Huddersfield to Longwood, I arrived home, much to the amazement of my parents and sisters. They had a dog, Rex, by this time — strangely he did not bark at my homecoming — as if he knew me, and he and I were always good friends.

Christmas (my first away from home) was spent at Fulford Barracks. On Christmas Eve Lieutenant White, the Bandmaster of the West Yorkshire Regiment had asked me if I would go with the band on that evening as they were to play carols on the green outside of York Minster. So just on midnight, with joy and some sadness (my brothers were out of the country) I sang solo 'Silent Night' with the gentle accompaniment of the band; a moment never to be forgotten.

The officers worked hard to give us all a good day. A lovely Christmas dinner was cooked by the mess staff — much credit was due to them — and the officers served us our meal amid much friendship and a few well meant catcalls.

Well remembered was a dance in the evening, when officers, NCOs and companies all joined in. Many songs of the day we parodied such as 'Elmer's Tune' — 'Listen, listen, isn't that the fire call you're missing? Hurry, scurry, put your respirator on while we sing this little song'.

As today — new words and phrases were used such as 'browned off' when we were a bit fed up or disgruntled and 'wizard' when things were good — nowadays it is 'brilliant' or 'cool', I understand.

We often had air-raid alarms — but worse came later on.

Soon after Christmas I was put on a rapid sergeant cadre with eleven other chosen corporals. This lasted three weeks and was very intense. We all tried our utmost to pass and this was the outcome, sergeant stripes were awarded to us on parade at the end of the course.

We continued to train dozens and dozens of new recruits with no weekends off, but I had a week's leave at the end of February.

After this time I was able to fulfil some promises of singing for the troops and was asked to join a group to do a show at Selby Hippodrome. I enjoyed this very much — a chance to escape routine. Permission first had to be obtained from the CO.

I returned from a leave to find that my dear friend, Doreen, had been posted. Remember it was a vital time in the war and we never met again. We did keep in touch for many years after the war bur very sadly Doreen was killed in a car accident some years later. As things are in war time — I am afraid that friends come and go and Helen Holdaway, a then corporal, became a friend along with Esme Burton, also a corporal, who was a gifted pianist, and accompanied my singing very often.

SELBY HIPPODROME
Proprietor — Mrs. Smith

7-30 p.m. on Sunday, 24th May, 1942

The RASCals
proudly present

"IT'S ON THE HOUSE"

a programme of Mirth and Melody

Dialogue by Peter Hansell, R.A.S.C.
Guy Anderson, R.A.S.C.
Stan. Barker, R.A.S.C.
Percy Butler, R.A.S.C.

Produced by
PERCY BUTLER, R.A.S.C.

Music arranged and directed by
Reg. Moore, R.A.S.C.

Stage Setting by Peter Hansell

Lighting Effects by Geo. Waterhouse

THE ENTIRE PRODUCTION
UNDER
THE PERSONAL SUPERVISION
OF 2/Lt. PERCY BUTLER, R.A.S.C.

Proceeds solely in aid of the R.A.S.C.
(Local) Troops Comforts Fund
(P.R.I. Account)

THE "BLUE PARROT" presenting JANE WHITEMAN'S floorshow
Park Avenue, NEW YORK.
"MUSIC AND MADNESS"

MORE FASCINATING SONGS & RHYTHM
Doreen Pickering
NOW WE WILL GO EAVESDROPPING ON
Sheila Butler and Tommy Taylor
BANJOISTICS - - George Cross
YOU SAY IT, I'LL PLAY IT
Reginald Moore
DRAMATIC RECITATION - Sheila Butler
THE EASTERN BROTHERS
Those Cads again
IMPRESSIONS BY JANE WHITEMAN
AND PERCY
X MORE LOVELY MELODIES X
Elsie Crossley

FASCINATING RHYTHM - Doreen Pickering
A LITTLE BIT OF NONSENSE
Tommy Taylor
ACCORDIAN HARMONY - Albert Owens
MUSIC AND MELODY
Reg. Moore and Harold Gilbert
THE GREEN EYE OF THE LITTLE YELLOW GOD
Stan Barker and Percy Butler
SELECTIONS FROM THE DESERT SONG
Albert Burn
THE EASTERN BROTHERS
Our Guest Artistes
X LOVELY MELODIES - Elsie Crossley X

MUSIC by REGINALD MOORE and his RASCals SUPER DANCE BAND
GRAND FINALE
Our HOSTESS for the evening - - - - Jane Whiteman

YOU NEVER KNOW JUST WHO MAY DROP IN DURING THE EVENING, OR WHAT MAY
HAPPEN; SO KEEP YOUR EARS AND EYES OPEN

ALL BODIES DELIVERED TO THE MORGUE FREE OF CHARGE.　FIRST CLASS CATERING

TWO PENCE
From York B.Ks.

The Selby Show — singing for the troops.

The war became more intensified and gas warfare was mooted.

I was sent for by the commanding officer (the CO), Miss Mordaunt who told me that she was sending me on a three week gas instructor course to Winterbourne Gunner on Salisbury Plain, so that I could on return, instruct the rest of the NCOs to pass it on to their platoons.

I departed like a pack horse with new kit — trousers and battledress in my holdall — along with complementary other items, i.e., boots, pullover, etc. The trousers/battledress had to be returned to stores on my return to York. Not only that, I had to carry on my back the usual respirator and steel helmet and in my spare hand two blankets! This should have been four blankets but I could not carry any more (still have the 'detail' order on this).

I arrived at a London railway station and had to report to the RTO (Railway Transport Officer — usually a sergeant, so I was equal there!). London was in the middle of a bombing raid and he helped me to a shelter for the next two hours or so; not a happy situation. Eventually the trains got going again and I found myself on a train going

Sgt. Crossley.

WRITTEN INSTRUCTIONS FOR G..S COURSE
AT ARMY GAS SCHOOL, WINTERBOURNE GUNNER.

You have been selected to attend

a Course which commences on the 25.5.42. You will report at the School between 1400 hrs. & 1700 on that date. Transport will meet you at the station. You will take blankets (4). Note books and pencils and Manual of Protection against gas & air-raids Pamphlet 1 & 2. You will be in possession of a return railway ticket, Course disperses on the 5.6.42.

N. Taylor.
                                        Sub.
O.C. No. 3 Recruit Coy.

Gas course instructions.

32

west out of London. Just in passing — I remember being amazed at the red-brown colour of the earth in the fields — it is almost black in the North.

I arrived at Salisbury and was met by the now familiar truck transport to take me out to the Gas Training Centre at Winterbourne Gunner (actually just outside the village) and I was given a room in a Nissen hut.

Whilst on this course on Saturday evenings a local lady (who owned an old bus!) ran us into Salisbury for four pennies each and returned us to camp (as long as she did not have to wait for us). We were there — it was a long walk back.

The course began the next day with lectures on the various war gases. During the course we had to 'sample' various gases by going through prepared huts. Not very pleasant, but then, not intended to be. We coughed and spluttered but there was no sympathy. One night at about 1.30 a.m. we were wakened and told to go on a night exercise when aircraft rained down 'something wet' which we were told was mustard gas and had to treat our exposed skin accordingly. Wonder what the 'something wet' was?

I passed my course with a first class (recorded in my pay book) and I returned to Fulford to instruct — first the officers and then the sergeants. I was officially in charge in case of an enemy gas raid. It made a break from drill instruction. By this time (and including my recent extra course) my Army pay had crept up somewhat and I now was being paid something like £2.10 shillings per week. A veritable fortune!

RSM Murfitt detailed twenty-four of us NCOs to form a special squad of drill demonstration. This was besides our squad training daily. He drilled us in the evenings on the barrack square doing advanced things like diagonal marching and many other forms, eventually with *no word of command* we completed a twenty minutes exercise.

There was to be a Special Army day at Selby and he took us there (by coach this time) and we put on our by now perfect demonstration on a *field* — the 'Lists' at Selby (more difficult than a firm barrack square). At the end of it The

Princess Royal — Princess Mary, inspected us and congratulated the RSM and ourselves. He was so pleased with us he actually smiled! I had a photo of this event but an unscrupulous person from Blackpool 'borrowed' this a few years ago and did not return it.

It was late springtime of 1942. We went to bed, as usual, but were wakened by the depot sirens at about midnight. We sergeants knew what we had to do and got our platoons quickly dressed and out of the buildings and took a roll call. This was a different alarm — and we were told that German bombers were imminent.

They certainly arrived that night and bombed Fulford Barracks and the City of York, including the station. I got my platoon and corporals under some solid stairs away from the billet blocks. It was quite petrifying but I had to keep the girls calm and comfort those who needed it. Some of them were only eighteen or nineteen — I was just twenty-one then but it was part of my duties. The raid seemed to go on for hours and it was almost Reveille time before we got the all-clear to emerge and be counted.

Next day I was instructed to take my squad out of the barracks (and out of the way!) on a route march. This I am afraid was an unsuccessful event as there were bomb craters around and about the barracks: enough to distress some of the younger ones, so after struggling to march around various side roads, we returned.

It was customary when the recruits were posted out in groups to their next destination, for them to be accompanied by a sergeant, who was responsible for all their documents and to deliver them and the girls safely.

I had a group of eight to take to London for Royal Signals training (mostly as telephonists). We arrived in London late afternoon where people were already making their way to subways for shelter — this being the time of high bomber raids. I reported to the RTO with my group where we were led to transport — this time something middle sized! It was getting dark and the sirens went — so as we were near to our destination the driver continued — I wanted to get the girls safely handed over.

We reached a large three storey building in Notting Hill to find as we entered that a lot of girls with signal flashes on their shoulders were coming down the stairs, to shelters. On passing one a voice said, "Hello Elsie — sorry can't stop" — and I was amazed to see my friend Kathleen Priestley from Parkwood. We had a quick hug and did not meet again until after the war. Happy moment in the middle of an air raid. I had to stay overnight because of the raid — the trains were stopped until the 'all-clear' went. These times were always a bit unnerving. I was glad to get out of London.

Very soon after our own bombing at Fulford (the Germans certainly knew where we were) our depot was moved en masse to a safer place. This transpired to be a girls' boarding school (public sector) at Harrogate. It was Queen Ethelburga's by name and consisted of several two storey buildings of red brick and some newly erected Nissen huts at the back in the field. It was situated about two miles out of the town in the hilly countryside.

This whole move was planned for and executed by Miss Tetley (Junior Commander then later Major) who was the depot's RQMS (she belonged to the family of 'Tetley' breweries). It was a brilliantly executed move, with a whole long train put on for us and we marched down to York Station. We lined up outside Harrogate Station on arrival, in companies and to the applause(!) of the crowds watching us, we marched with our kit the two miles to our new home.

CHAPTER 4

Ethelburga's

Come inside to Ethelburga's — come inside.
You really ought to have more sense.
Working for a living — take my tip —
Join the ATS and become a part of it —
You get your meals regular —
And two new suits besides
Thirty bob a week
No kids to keep —
Come inside to Ethelburga's — come inside.

I do not know who devised the song but we sang it together at a Company Concert there and on route marches.

Up hill for the last mile on our march to our new home we were allowed a break of ten minutes. The first view of Ethelburga's was of three or four two storied red brick buildings, surrounded by gardens/lawn — not eight foot walls!

We in no. 3 Company were allocated some newly erected Nissen huts to the rear of the school across what had been the playing fields. I had a good corporal there — Margaret Wilcocks from Liverpool. She was most reliable in her help with my platoon. Once between intakes we had both a thirty-six hour pass, so we took a train and went to visit her parents at Liverpool where we spent a happy, if short weekend.

Our sergeants' quarters were in the main block — separate from the lower ranks as ever — for discipline's sake.

Queen Ethelburga's, Harrogate.

NCOs No.3 Coy. Back row from left: Joy, Liz, Elsie, RSM, CSM, Ivy. Front: Margaret, Ethel, Sheila, Helen.

There were three of us in our room — Helen Holdaway, Ivy Burwood and myself. We became firm friends.

Unfortunately our Junior Commander Miss Burnett (now Taylor) and our helpful CSM had been posted elsewhere and we had a new officer and a CSM. The CSM was of the 'old school' had served at the end of the 1st World War and was therefore much older than us — must have been middle or late forties. She never seemed to like our smart appearance — well trained attitude that we had and was in fact something of a bully and tyrant at times. We kept out of her way as much as possible.

Sixteen recruits destined for ack-ack were to be taken to Norwich for their next training. Helen and I were detailed to take them. As senior I was given charge of their documents and we got on our way. Air raids were quite numerous at that time and we found that we had to change trains several times — not an easy task with sixteen excited recruits and all their kit.

Nevertheless we eventually arrived at Norwich Station and I reported to the RTO — as usual. It was early evening — coming dusk and we were able to hand over documents and girls to an officer and sergeant of the RA. The RTO said, "I am afraid that we are getting heavy raids here at present and no more trains will be running tonight."

As we had nowhere to stay he gave us the key to his hut just outside the station where there were bunk beds. We made our way there but Helen — a bit of a psychic one said, "I do not feel right here and cannot sleep in this place." So we moved out — could not find the RTO so kept the key until morning.

Walking away from the town, after about one and a half miles, we came across a pub and asked the landlord if he had a spare room. "Yes" he said "but my young daughter has measles if you don't mind that." We thought anywhere was better than bombs. There was a severe raid in and around Norwich that night. We slept little.

We were up the next morning and off at 6.30 to walk back to the station to find quite some devastation. The RTO fell on us with relief. He thought we were dead as the hut

Sergeants' mess, No.2 ATS, TC.
Elsie, ninth from right, middle row.

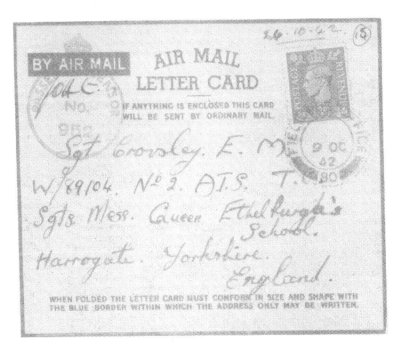

Air Mail from author's brother Harold in the Middle East.

and its area had had a direct hit! It was a pair of very sober sergeants who made their return journey to Harrogate. Thankful indeed.

I haven't mentioned food rations on these escorted duties — but it was always thick sandwiches of corned beef. I had enough. I still cannot eat a corned beef sandwich!

When we had a Saturday free, Helen and I used to go into Harrogate (no buses we had to walk) and as we were sergeants, we were now allowed out until 12.00 midnight on Saturdays, so we were able to go to dances. We used to have tea in the crypt of a church — tea being provided (for about 9d) by the WI, I think.

On one of these outings we found a dance taking place at one of the large (posh!) hotels. Always turned out smartly, we found two RAF corporals taking an interest in us. They were both charming and well mannered and friendships developed — myself with Tom and Helen with Pat.

Some weeks later we had a 'do' in our sergeants' mess and our kind RSM Scarborough allowed us to invite them. A fact which did not go down well with our Coy CSM — but she could not overrule the RSM.

Tom and I continued with just a happy friendship — although on one occasion he visited at my home quite unexpectedly, whilst I was on leave. He often bought me books on poetry — some of which I still have. In recent times we had discovered each others' address and although I am widowed and he a widower we found that we are able to correspond from time to time. Still good friends.

Helen fell deeply in love with Pat and was devastated when the boys were posted away — to India it transpired later. Going a bit ahead — Helen never married and we kept in touch all the years. Again — sadly I lost a friend as she died in 1978 of a brain tumour.

Since writing this account and quite recently, Tom, after a very active life, became ill. He rang me with one of his happy telephone calls — but during it was taken ill quite suddenly. He was (his daughter informed me) taken to hospital and died after a few days, just prior to his birthday in January 2003. I shall miss his bright voice and long friendship of over sixty years.

During my time at Ethelburga's training continued. I still sang at Company Concerts. Especially a 'classy' one at the men's barracks at Penny Pot Lane (about half a mile up the road). I still have the programme for this concert and many others with my name firmly in print. I remember one of my songs this time was, "Solveigs Song".

Two former pupils of Queen Ethelburga's joined our company, Sheila Campbell and Liz Hirsch. It must have been very strange for them.

I was senior sergeant in our company and one of the senior in the training centre. One day the commanding officer, Miss Mordaunt, sent for me. "There are two Bermudan girls coming to join us in a few days time as potential officers. I want you to take them under your wing and train them as such, to prepare them for officer training," she said. This was a pleasant change from recruits and I happily got on with it. (Ref. Note: a CO is the commanding officer of a whole regiment, an OC is the officer commanding a company within a regiment.)

There was a small church within the school grounds and I formed a choir of six girls to sing there and at services on Church Parade.

About six months after being at Queen Ethelburga's I fell foul of the CSM — she was cutting me out of good duties and giving me unwanted ones. We had a blazing row and I complained to the RSM (Miss Scarborough) of her attitude towards me, this was the correct procedure. This concluded with the CSM being reprimanded by the CO. It passed with time.

It became clear that the recruits were thinning out. When I think back I must have personally trained — at the rate of about thirty-six per month — about 700 recruits over a period of about two years (allowing for leaves).

It was announced that we were to have a 'General' Inspection. This obviously meant that our training centre was due for closure. It meant what it said and urgent preparation went forward with a complete rehearsal before the day.

It happened to be Field Marshal Sir William Slim who came to inspect each and every one of us permanent staff. I think we were pleased that someone so important visited us and we were surprised at his kindliness and his quite small stature. The day went well. I was recently taken to London on a visit by my family and we found the statue of Field Marshal Slim. I had, of course, to have my photo taken beside this great man!

As the year went on and the Christmas concert of 1942 came and went the recruits were almost in short supply and I became restless for something more useful and interesting to do. Some training did continue. I spoke with the RSM about it who said that she would look into it for something suitable, but it might be some time, as I was still needed there.

Eventually an interesting posting came up to learn about vehicle parts, vehicle transport and then to tanks. "Was I interested?" I quickly volunteered for this new life in the Army and was duly posted to Derby, to Normanton Barracks, in late Autumn.

A recent photo of the author at the statue of Field Marshal Slim in London.

42

CHAPTER 5

Motor Transport and Tank Training

I arrived at Normanton Barracks, Derby to an entirely different life. I was there to learn not to instruct and I was full of anticipation.

I shared a room with a sergeant who was on the clerical side there and I was taken out to a COD depot where vehicle parts were assembled — checked — accounted for and dispatched to units all over the UK. I had to learn the 'paperwork'.

After a couple of weeks there in this huge, long building I saw an ATS private trying to catch my eye and as I went down the lines to her I recognised her as my eldest brother's new bride from Glasgow. We had a quick hug and a kiss — not allowed to linger — she was a typist on special duties. She told me in later years that it took a long time to live down — 'the sergeant giving her a hug!'

Before long a notice went up asking for 'talent' for a Depot Show. I volunteered my name and Subaltern (ATS) H. Lewis came to see me. She seemed pleased that I was willing to join in and I found myself with the main singing part in the show, which we put on at the men's barracks down the road where they had a huge hall with stage.

We called the show "The COD Optimists" (have programme). One of the items involved me leading a group of 'presumed' choristers — all of us dressed in white — from the back of the hall, down through the audience to the stage. It was very impressive and I was singing 'Ave

Maria' whilst the girls hummed the tune.

After the show the male RSM of the Grenadier Guards came round to us to thank us and invited us all to supper in the mess. This was Bill. I suppose we fell in love and it became one of the happiest periods of my service.

Just after Christmas we put on a late pantomime with some of the Army joining in the cast. Wonderful characters. It was Aladdin and I was Princess Balroubadour. I have a photo of us all and the programme.

Bill and I met when we could — duties allowing and I spent many most happy evenings in the sergeants' mess with him and occasionally a tea out on a Saturday in Derby, with a film show.

This period was not without air raids as we were close to the Rolls-Royce engines factory and many nights were spent out of bed and into group safe places. It was hard some days to concentrate on vehicle parts following one of these nights. Yes! fear did enter into it sometimes and drained the energy.

My time then drew to a close and Bill put on a farewell party for me in the mess. I still have the invitation — he always did things correctly! We had a lovely but very sad evening, but remember it was wartime and attachments and partings were the order of the day.

My next sojourn and final part of my motor transport and tank training was to be in Scotland. I remember feeling so very sad and quietly shedding some tears on my train journey up to Glasgow. Bill was later posted abroad. I missed him and still keep his photo.

My next five or six weeks were at Rouken Glen, near Glasgow. We were in a large old house and the platoon was in Nissen huts in adjoining grounds.

I was taken every day to the motor transport depot where Army vehicles of all kinds were in daily use and repair. Here I had to learn how and to where they were issued and become familiar with all types of documentation. Having arrived there and knowing that it was another 'step' I put my mind to it. At least we were not getting any air raids.

C.O.D. But A Real Treat

The first performance of "The C.O.D.-Optimists," a newly formed variety show by A.T.S. members of an Ordnance Depot, was given last night.

Considering that rehearsals began only three weeks ago under its producer Subaltern Hylda Lewis, who escaped from Italy after the outbreak of war, an attractive and efficient commere, the show was of exceptionally high quality and standard.

The costumes were designed and made at the camp by Senior Commanders R. M. Villiers-Stuart and P. Tetley.

Cleverly disguised netball posts and the depot's post-box formed part of the show's most impressive s c e n e, "Gounod Time." Sergeant E. M. Crossley gave a beautiful rendering of "Ave Maria" with a chorus of six of the company dressed as choristers.

"A Night in Paris" gave L/Cpl. I. Findlay as "Apache" and Pte. M. Tucker as "Mimi" the opportunity for a clever dancing display and "Now This Blooming War Is Over," presented entirely by the officers, was very successful with its pointed repartee.

L/Cpl. N. Lamer danced the steps which won for her the title North of England Tap Dancing Champion.

A review of the C.O.D. concert.

NO. 8 BATTALION R.A.O.C.

AND

DERBY C.O.D. GROUP A.T.S

GRAND XMAS PANTOMIME

& HIS WONDERFUL LAMP. L.V.6

Aladdin programme.

The cast of Aladdin — author in centre of middle row.

C A S T

ALADDIN .... L/CPL. FINDLEY A.T.S.
PRINCESS BALROUBADOUR.......... SGT. CROSSLEY A.T.S.
WIDOW TWANKEY....................... SGT. HATHAWAY R.A.O.C.
W.O.I. OF CHINA........................... PTE. STRONACH R.A.O.C.
ABANAZAR THE MAGICIAN......... PTE. MAY R.A.O.C.
MINISTER OF INTERIOR................ PTE. APPLETON R.A.O.C.
MINISTER OF INTERIOR................ PTE. NISBET R.A.O.C.
MINISTER OF ULTERIOR................ SGT. FIRTH R.A.O.C.
SLAVE OF THE RING...................... L/CPL. PICKETT R.A.O.C.
SLAVE OF THE LAMP..................... PTE. MATHIESON R.A.O.C.
WISHEE WASHEE......................... MASTER PHILIP MILLER

A.T.S. DANCE TROUPE TRAINED BY L/CPL. LAKER A.T.S.

SGT. FARNHAM	PTE. BURNETT
PTE. EWART	PTE. PERERA
PTE. RITCHIE	PTE. COPE

CHORUS

L/CPL. WEBSTER (A.T.S.)	PTE. DESBOROUGH (A.T.S)	PTE. EVANS (A.T.S)
PTE. PHILLIPS (A.T.S)	PTE. BARRETT (A.T.S.)	CPL. SUGDEN (R.A.O.C.)
	PTE. HOWELLS (R.A.O.C.)	

JOAN HEDLEY'S JUVENILES

BETTY DALE	BETTY FUDLEY	ELSIE CHEETHAM
MARJORIE DYER	P.T ALLSOPP	JOAN TAYLOR
	NANCY TONES	

DEVISED AND PRODUCED BY LIEUT. H.M. SMITH R.A.O.C.

SCENE ONE   THE C.O.D. HOOFLING, CHINA
"I'm a W.O.I. of China"   PTE. STRONACH
"I Love to sing"   L/CPL. FINDLEY & DANCE TROUPE

SCENE TWO   TWANKEY'S LAUNDRY
"Rub-a-dub-dub"   DANCE TROUPE & CHORUS
"He led me up the garden"   SGT. HATHAWAY

SCENE THREE   A CHINESE GARDEN
Duet "Land of Willow Pattern Plate"   SGT. CROSSLEY & L/CPL. FINDLEY
"Three married Martyrs"   SGT. FIRTH
                                 PTE. APPLETON
                                 PTE. NISBET

SCENE FOUR   OUTSIDE THE CAVE

SCENE FIVE   INSIDE THE CAVE
"Genii of the Magic ..."   The Juveniles
"Little men with feathers"   L/CPL. BENNETT
                                 L/CPL. FINDLEY
"Tap-tap"

SCENE SIX   TWANKEY'S KITCHEN
Transformation scene
"Put your arms around me honey" Full company

TEN MINUTES INTERVAL

SCENE SEVEN
"The World is Mine Tonight"   SGT. CROSSLEY
"I'm going to see you today"   PTE. DESBOROUGH

SCENE EIGHT   AFRICA
"SGT. MAJOR'S Serenade"   PTE. EVANS
                                 SGT. FIRTH
                                 PTE. APPLETON
                                 Ptes. Ritchie &
                                 Perera & Chorus
"Gertie from Bizerte"   PTE. NISBET
"Myself when young"   SGT. FIRTH
                                 SGT. HATHAWAY
"Up-two-three" "Down-two-three" L/CPL. FINDLEY
                                 L/CPL. PICKETT
                 Ptes. Appleton, Mathieson & Stronach

SCENE NINE   INSIDE THE PALACE
"My heart and I"   SGT. CROSSLEY
"If I had my way"   Full company

F I N A L E

G O D   S A V E   T H E   K I N G

The Orchestra under the direction of Sergeant L. RAINE

1st Violins	(Cpl. Murphy	2nd Violin	Cpl. Leonard
	(Pte. Gompers	Viola	Pte. King
Cello	Pte. White	Bass	Cpl. Johnstone
Flute	L/Cpl Kenny	Clarinet	Cpl. Naden
Trumpets	(Sgt. Trevorrow	Trombone	Pte. Coleman
	(L/Cpl. Craig	Drums & Effects	Pte. Strickland
Piano	Ptes. Atkinson & Last	Saxophone	Pte. Lanton

Aladdin programme.

Bill and the party invitation he sent Elsie.

The author in a borrowed kilt at Rouken Glen.

I found that I had the kindest and most considerate ATS CSM (CSM Schwabe) that it was possible to have. There were only five of us in the sergeants' mess. Two FANYS, our CSM, one other ATS sergeant (Margaret) and myself. We shared equally the chores of duties — night watch etc., and were happy together.

Bet Schwabe asked me to 'smarten up' the platoon with a bit of drill every other day. There were about thirty girls. I did this happily and they responded when they realised that I knew what I was doing! I gave them drill instruction or a short march frequently — sometimes in the evening. Life was never dull — there was always duty to be done.

After a couple of weeks I got them together to rehearse for a concert, which seemed to be appreciated by all. It was a change for the ATS there.

On the third Saturday I was there CSM Schwabe and Margaret and myself decided to go to a show and tea out in Glasgow. We were twelve miles away and the lovely bus company allowed us to travel all that way for one penny each.

The evenings were becoming longer and after a very late tea we walked down Sauchiehall Street to our bus stop. There we chatted and waited until suddenly someone put a hand on my arm and said, "Elsie!" I could not believe my eyes — it was my eldest brother Norman. I do not know who was the most surprised. He was duly introduced to my two friends and asked me if I could spend the following day, Sunday, with him. I was on duty.

My CSM said, "Of course you can go. I will rearrange the duty."

Norman came out early to our billet to pick me up and we travelled all the way by bus — a penny on each bus for me — to Loch Lomond. We sat upstairs on the bus and along with us was a crowd (perhaps seven or eight) of youngsters aged about sixteen. They sang 'Hail Caledonia' at the top of their voices — it all helped to make my day memorable. At Loch Lomond Norman took out a boat for us and rowed me to the little island in the middle of the loch. On return we had a meal at the cafe and eventually returned to Glasgow and Rouken Glen. I no longer have my dear brother, but I shall never forget the lovely day we spent together. He often spoke about it in later years.

One of the girls invited me to tea at her home (she lived about ten miles away nearer the city). Her mother was so kind to me — she had made scones, scotch pancakes and fruit cake, all out of their meagre rations. I was most touched at the hospitality. It was a great pleasure to be so welcomed. Do not ever decry the Scots. They are generous and kind.

A few days later my posting to my new unit came through. My instructions were to go by train to Bristol where I would be met. Along with me was posted a group of ATS privates, drivers, maintenance and office staff, who were in my care until we reached Bristol where the girls were met by an NCO from 'F' Company. They were good girls and did not cause me any undue anxiety on the long journey — except at Manchester Station. There one of them hopped off the train to buy cakes for the rest of the girls, from the Women's Institute stall on the platform. I am pleased to say that we had quite a long wait and she returned with her bag of 'goodies' in good time.

A few days after my arrival at Bristol I received a letter from CSM Schwabe thanking me for the work I did for her platoon. I still have the letter.

I had come a long way from the raw recruit at York. It was April 1944 and I had now three red chevrons on my sleeve for long service and extra top passes in instruction, gas warfare, motor transport parts plus technical knowledge, and of course quite a few increments in my pay on the way. I was now an experienced and well qualified soldier. A far different person from the young choir girl at Parkwood Chapel.

CHAPTER 6

ATS Southern Command

My posting was to 31st AFV (Armoured Fighting Vehicles — tanks). Via 'F' Coy. ATS Southern Command.

It was a long day and we did not arrive at Temple Meads, Bristol until late evening. I got the girls off the train with all our kit and reported (as usual) to the RTO. As the girls (ATS) were for a separate unit there was an ATS corporal waiting for them and I handed them and their documents over to her.

There was a driver and a 15-cwt truck waiting for me to take me to my new posting. It was a good two to three mile drive through Bristol — passing the cathedral on the way I saw much bomb damage in the city and the driver said yes, they were getting their fair share of air raids. We continued up White Ladies Road up hill to Clifton Downs and the residential part of Bristol.

Eventually he drove up a short drive to a very large old house which, he informed me was *next to the tank park,* at Sea Walls. I alighted from the truck and the driver helped me off with my kit. Looking up at the numerous windows I saw faces watching me. Knowing that these were going to be my girls — I gave them a friendly wave and I hope a big smile. Good to start off on the right foot.

The door opened and there waiting for me was my new officer Subaltern Margaret Naish. "Thank goodness you have arrived safely," she said. "We have been having air raids and I hoped you would be here before dark." She had allocated a large front first floor room to me. It seemed huge with its single iron bed, a wardrobe and a dressing table

51

(what luxury). The floors were of course just wood and I could see that I would have my time cut out to keep the floor dusted! We got on well from the start. She told me that she was new to the unit (and a new officer I guessed!) and was perhaps going to rely on my help and experience. She showed me where the sergeants' mess was for the Tank Unit — just inside the depot about fifty yards from the billet. A gap had been made in the dividing hedge, which we all used! Subaltern Naish also said would I report to the captain commanding the Tank Unit the following morning at 9.00 a.m.

After she left me I unpacked (did not take long!) and made my way to the sergeants' mess. There I found waiting for me my working companions for the future — a male CSM and two male sergeants. Four of us made up this group and we were between us to run the depot. They welcomed me warmly and I found them to be friendly and helpful. (Later on more senior NCOs arrived.)

After an hour or so I went back to my billet and strange room. I thought time enough for the girls tomorrow. It had been a long day.

The following morning I made myself smart and after breakfast in the mess, was taken by the CSM to see Captain Guscott. I think he was amazed to see the smart salute and stood to his feet. We shook hands — most unusual — and he asked me to sit, so that he could explain what my job was all about and to tell me that on no account was I to write home or anywhere about the job in hand. We were to help in preparing tanks for a landing in France — date to be disclosed later. The ATS were to replace as many men as possible to relieve them for active service.

So I had to sort out the girls for clerical work, driving trucks, checking tanks, checking gun parts on the tanks and checking to see that replacements were complete for the Bren guns 303s attached to the tanks. They were to be mainly classed as store women so that their jobs would not be made public in any way. I made sure that they got extra pay for this. Caption Guscott knew that this was my first experience of a working company and said that if I had any problems to go to him ONLY. He then took me on a

Elsie and the two other original NCOs at Bristol.

Elsie walking back to her billet across the downs, Bristol.

tour of the depot and I was shown the different tanks and carriers which were waiting to be checked. I could see that the girls' uniforms (and mine) were not suited to this kind of job and I asked right away for working clothing.

Returning to the billet I called out the ATS on to parade and took a roll call. They were all new there and had come from various parts of the country. I explained to them what was to happen and told them that after lunch in their mess, to parade, and I would take them to stores to be kitted out suitably. Myself included.

So we finished up that day with trousers and battledress top, ankle gaiters (the ground was soft and muddy in parts), boots and a leather sleeveless jerkin each. The trousers had to be pressed (and the top) and the gaiters blancoed and boots cleaned every day. This, I insisted on — discipline had to be maintained and I duly inspected every morning.

As it was a working unit — there were thirty-six allocated to the depot — I had a corporal clerk, a depot corporal and a lance corporal to help along. I still have a nominal roll of them all.

I had to check that they were all on duty (morning parade and roll call at 7.30). All indoors at lights out and see to such morning duties as sick parade, problems, leaves when due and a certain amount of PE when time permitted — at least once a week. So to this end we formed a netball team and a reserve and I refereed — hopefully doing all the right things. But this came later.

I was in at the 'deep end' and it was necessary to get the girls to work on their jobs. With the help of the men NCOs we got them sorted out and fortunately the ATS were well suited to their various new jobs and got on with them. It was hard work and they finished the days tired and dirty. I had of course to learn something about all their jobs so that I was working too, beside keeping an eye on them for any excess fatigue.

Tanks which were completed and checked and fitted out with necessary spares, were taken in convoys of six across the downs under the beautiful Clifton Suspension Bridge

NOMINAL ROLL A.T.S. 31. AFV DEPOT

S/T. CROSSLEY E.M. — IN CHARGE OF DEPOT A.T.S.
Sgt. .... — STORE...... - (KIT STORES)
CPL. DAVIES MEA... — CLERK - (TECH A.D.)
L/Cpl. IVYLIE.. I.M. — STOREWOMAN - (CHECKER)
Pte. BARBIERI. M.R. — (")
" BOWN. E.M. — (MAINTENANCE)
" BRADBURY. B. — (")
" CALLAGHAN. M. — CLERK.
" COOPER. C. — STOREWOMAN - (MAINTENANCE)
" COOPER. D.L. — CLERK - (DEPOT DRIVING LICENSE)
" COOKE. A. — STOREWOMAN - (MAINTENANCE)
Sub. CUENEY. P. — CLERK (& MESS ORDERLY)
" ELLIOTT. M. — STOREWOMAN - (CHECKER)
" FERGUSON. I.M. — CLERK. - (VOUCHER PREP)
" FORRESTER. M.J. — STOREWOMAN - (CHECKER)
" GARDNER. ...... — " - (MAINTENANCE)
" HARRIS. ...... — ( )
" HIBBERT. ...... — ( )
" HOLT. T. E. — DRIVER.
" HARVEY. F. — STOREWOMAN - (MAINTENANCE)
" JONES. A.E. — ( )
" LAPPAGE. E. — STOREWOMAN - (CHECKER)
" McHUGH. ME. — DRIVER.
" MORGAN. K.A. — CLERK.

" MEIER. C. — DRIVER.
" OUGH. A. — DRIVER.
" RADLEY. M. — STOREWOMAN - (MAINTENANCE)
" RAYNES. O. — CLERK - chaplain (but les ...)
" RENSHAW. E. — STOREWOMAN - (MAIN TEX ARTE)
" SMITH. C. — (QM STORE?)
" SMITH. D. — CLERK.
" STEWART. M. — STOREWOMAN - (CHECKER)
" SPEDDING. F. — (PACKING & ...)
" WELDING. J. — CLERK - (PAY.)
" WESTON. J. — STOREWOMAN - (MT.C)
" WOOD. J. — CLERK.
" WYMAN. G. — DRIVER. 3.
POWELL A.
" BOSS. K.M. — MESS ORDERLY
" LARKINS. V.
" DAVY. C.

TOTAL (TECHNICAL)
STOREWOMEN. 21.
CLERKS. 10.
DRIVERS. 5.

E.J. Crosby
A.T.S.

The ATS netball team — author in the middle of back row.

A quick respite from the tanks — author front right.

(which was very close to us) and along the lower road to the docks of Avonmouth. There was in each tank a driver (usually a male NCO) and an observer. As some of the men were beginning to leave us, the girls often used to take their place as observer at the front of the tank — head and shoulders above (complete with steel helmet). They looked on this as a treat — a reward for their hard work on that particular tank.

I often used to be in the front tank — leading, as I was then responsible for the tanks' documents to be handed over at port. People used to watch us pass by (they could hardly help this as the tracks made such a noise and the heavy engines drowned most sounds) but I do remember a voice shouting — "It's a girl!" So I gave a wave. I am afraid on looking back, that the tank tracks made a ruin of the downs and spoilt road surfaces. So! Such was the price of FREEDOM.

We had an NCOs' meeting every three days, headed by the CO of the 31st AFV. He kept us up to date with events and the new movement of tanks to be taken to the South Coast. It was now halfway through May 1944 and we knew that something was imminent. All the unit ATS and men were working on the tanks and troop carriers (Staghounds) from 7.30 in the morning until 9.00 p.m. or even after at night.

Those girls were so good. No one complained and throughout all my time there I *never* had one girl go AWOL. All leave was stopped and we were to instruct the platoon not to mention anything of our work in their letters home. It poured with rain. We were ankle deep in mud in parts of the depot.

During this time the Salvation Army came up to the depot twice a day with buns and hot drinks to give to us all. Breaks were given for meals and an hour rest in the afternoon, in relays. The rain continued. We were at last issued with gumboots.

I did escort duty with groups of tanks — some of these on transporters to get them down to the South Coast which of course was still being bombed by enemy aircraft.

CHAPTER 7

Channel Crossings

6th June, 1944, this was the day we had all been working towards. We were called on parade in the evening and addressed by the CO to tell us what had happened and he praised thoroughly the jobs that the girls had done. But, as he said, it could not stop and we had to go on with the work.

As I have written, I had been doing escort duty with tanks to Avonmouth docks and to the South Coast, but more drivers for the tanks were needed for Normandy. It was on the Friday morning after D-day that the CO sent for me. As I already knew we had six tanks ready to go out so I assumed it was to go with them. He said that he needed me to take charge of their documents and see them *this time, over to France*, but of course, being ATS I was required to *volunteer* for my overseas duty. Very readily I said, "Yes," and signed a form to this effect.

Now the shock. "Get ready right away — you have one hour," he said and advised me to tell my corporal to take charge of the girls as I was going on 'compassionate weekend leave' until Monday or Tuesday.

The tanks, each with a driver and navigator as crew, were duly loaded at the edge of the depot onto transporters as we were to go direct to Portsmouth — this was quicker with transporters and less road destroying.

I was back in the CO's office in time with only my respirator and steel helmet and full working kit. There waiting for me was a pack of sandwiches and the documents. I was given full instructions not to let these documents leave my person, and how to board the ship, and what to do on the other side! Then quietly and without fuss was told to go to the main gate where a 15-cwt truck was waiting for me with our depot captain as driver.

I got in quickly. There were certain 'spares' in the back in case of any problems with the tanks. We drew away for a short distance to allow for the tanks to be completely loaded and secured, and we set off leading. I had had no time to think until now.

"OK?" asked the captain.

"Yes Sir," I replied.

He had our route planned well as of course there were no signposts remaining (all removed for wartime), and with the slow moving transporters we had to have a half-way break at an Army depot on the way; the navigators taking their break first with the officer in charge, followed by me with the drivers.

On reaching the outskirts of Portsmouth I felt my stomach tightening and a wave of apprehension came over me. What had I let myself in for?

After that it was all 'go'. We arrived, took our turn — had last instructions from 'Capt Jack' and I watched with worry whilst my tanks were loaded on board. As they were chained and secured the drivers and the few navigators, only two (one in the first and me in the last) came to stand with me. They trusted me and I, them, come what may. We found a corner to call our own and to return to after visiting toilets and finding something to drink, we made it our rendezvous until sailing time when I said that except in emergency we must stay together. It was now very dark and way after midnight, so we tried to get a 'kip'. No lights were shown on sailing and I must admit to feeling apprehension again, but could not show it — the 'boys' thought they were looking after me.

I suppose, (in retrospect), it was not a bad crossing, not rough and the weather so much better than the previous week had been. I think we were all constantly wondering if we would be bombed and a few sick jokes were muttered;

it kept the spirits up a little. A long night but before dawn we were told to return to our tanks ready for disembarkation, at Arromanches. Since the Mulberry Harbour was still under construction it was necessary to transfer the tanks, at sea, to smaller landing craft that could be beached safely to allow the tanks to be driven ashore. I watched this transfer with apprehension, I did not want to lose any of my tanks during this operation, but thankfully, it all went off satisfactorily.

Dawn! and I found myself squashed into a small powered boat along with others 'on foot' to do the last 100 yards or so to shore. It looked frightening and like bedlam — but was in fact well organised by the beach marshal. I managed to get to him and showed him my documents. Another sergeant escorted me to the officer in charge tanks to whom I was able to hand over the documents after the tanks I had escorted had been duly inspected and the drivers vetted. (On the third visit landing was much easier as the Mulberry Harbour had been completed and was in operation.)

I was by now, cold, tired, hungry (nothing to eat or drink on the crossing) and very apprehensive. Having handed over my tanks and wishing the drivers 'God Speed' and having a moment to think I began to wonder how I was to return to England. I 'collared' an Army sergeant who was on beach duty. He referred me to a 'Return to England' section to register and I was told to hang about — probably for about a couple of hours or so, and go and get a drink and a 'bite' but not to wander off — as if I dare.

Eventually, just before dark, I was called to be ready to embark. Again, a small boat was to take me, and some others, to a bigger ship, anchored off shore, which was going to return to England at nightfall (relief to find that I was not forgotten).

It was another worrying time (waiting to be boarded) as German aircraft were still bombing along the coast. Eventually I was boarded and the ship set sail in complete darkness, no lights to be shown. It was not a very comfortable trip, there were no facilities for food or drink and no accommodation was available on board (this was not a Channel ferry). I managed to find a coil of rope on which to sit during the crossing. Eventually the ship reached England, what a relief. Again disembarking I was guided (or led) by voices to report to the returning officer and was included in a wait for transport returning to Gloucestershire — which did drop me off at 31st AFV Depot, Bristol — many hours later.

I reported to my CO (Major Vaughan) only to be told rest for a couple of days as I was to return with the next convoy which was almost ready. Tanks were needed desperately and I had two more escort duties following quickly.

On my third visit I was not so lucky. The, by now, familiar routine of reaching France and disembarkation completed, having despatched my tanks, drivers, and documents, I was told by the beach marshal that nothing was returning to England for at least twenty-four hours as bombing raids were expected from the Germans. So I was found a place to sleep for the night in a tent with a couple of ATS corporals, who were employed as cooks for the Army, the usual 'truckle' bed, three 'biscuits' (these made up a mattress) and a couple of blankets, and I hoped that I might get some sleep. This was impossible and word went around that there was an impending air raid by German bombers.

I went outside the tent and could hear aircraft approaching. No shelter of course — just 'pot luck'. The aircraft was getting closer and the duty sergeant shouted, "Down! Down! Down!" One didn't hesitate, just fell flat. The next moment a bomb had exploded nearby, and pieces of shrapnel had hit my face. One piece hit my mouth and broke a couple of teeth — another piece hit high on my left cheekbone. There was blood of course and all I could think of was that, I hoped, my eye was all right.

I was soon picked up and taken to the field dressing station for treatment and after my anxious questioning was reassured that my eye was OK. However, that piece of shrapnel had damaged my cheekbone. I still have the small dent in my left cheek and can feel the dent in the bone. It was a frightening experience — over very quickly and all the courage in the world does not make it less so. I recently read somewhere "Courage isn't being fearless — courage is being afraid and going on".

With no choice in the matter I was kept for a further twenty-four hours then found a passage back home.

On returning to the depot at Bristol I was detailed to a few days in a 'house-rest-hospital' nearby. This did not please me greatly — I was anxious to be back on duty and did not feel ill.

Following this I discovered that my mother had written to the CO to enquire if I was alright as I had not written home for two or three weeks — NO COMMENT!

After this I carried out three more escort journeys by which time there were a few more male sergeants available to take over the duty and I was able to turn my attention once again to the work at 31st AFV Depot and my girls. An unforgettable time in my Army life.

In no time at all it seemed damaged tanks were being returned to us battered and bruised and needing repair and rechecking. They also had to be cleaned out which was, in some cases, a bit daunting as men had been injured in them.

After a few weeks we had a visit from the director of the ATS, Chief Controller L. V. Whateley CBE to thank us all and inspect the work the ATS were doing (I have a photo of this).

American tanks began to arrive in the depot — Shermans. They had been brought over the Atlantic in grain ships — I suppose as camouflage. Anyway — the various crevasses and spaces were filled with corn and, not wanting to waste anything, I asked the girls to collect what they could and fill bags with it. It had a purpose! My dad had a few hens in a spare bit of ground and had not been able to get much grain for them for a long time. I put this lot in my kitbag and when I got leave (my first for about five months) I took the grain home with me. Dad gave me some eggs to bring back to the girls concerned and they were so pleased (we only ever had one egg per month in rations). They managed, somehow, to cook the eggs.

We were now back to almost normal hours of duty and

GIRL TANK MECHANICS, engaged in re-servicing armoured vehicles, explain features of th work to Chief Controller L. V. L. E. Whateley, C.B.E., Director of A.T.S., who paid a visit t Bristol area yesterday.

L. V. Whateley's inspection — the author is just visible between the two officers on the left.

various talks, on such things as Current Affairs, were given us.

On a leave home about this time (there were still air raids taking place), I decided to go on an overnight train to give me an extra few hours at home in Huddersfield. So I boarded a train at Bristol Temple Meads which was full of Canadian soldiers. There were no seats available and I was not going to squash into a compartment (in those days a compartment held about eight to ten people) with them. So I stayed in the corridor along with standing soldiers. They were so kind, they made me a seat with their kit bags and before the train left Bristol one of them hopped off the train to get me a hot drink. It was a weird journey through the night and the train stopped just outside Birmingham. We knew there was an air raid in progress and could see fires starting up. It was a good thing we were stopped there, hoping the bombers did not see our train — it was full of troops. We probably waited there for two to three hours before continuing to Staley Bridge near Manchester. There I changed trains — after thanking my kindly escorts — and arrived home tired and weary at about 9.30 a.m. I felt the lack of music and wanted to sing again.

Home on leave, Elsie, sisters Dora and Irene, her mother and Rex.

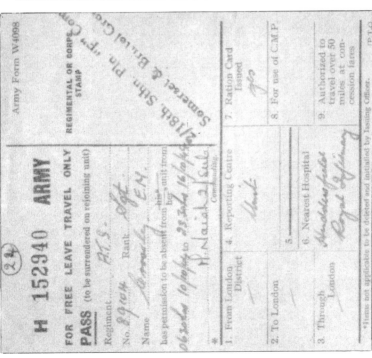

A leave pass.

CHAPTER 8

Sergeant, 'Mother' and Entertainer

Work at the depot continued, but there was now no urgency. A few romances blossomed. One couple married. Another couple became engaged and were married at the end of hostilities. Then a third couple — a pretty blonde girl and her tank driver were unfortunately parted as he was posted away. The night before he left was barrack night (all indoors) when someone came to me and said could Mary go out for half an hour to say goodbye to Tash (his nickname). I trusted her not to make off and she returned safely. I hoped they married later — they were very much in love.

Captain Guscott invited me out for an evening to a 'local' and skittle alley. We enjoyed the break and he told me of his wedding plans to take place in a few months time.

The sergeants' mess was now full — sergeants etc. being returned from other duties. There was one particularly offensive CSM. I could not bear to be near him — so I transferred my meals to the HQ sergeants' mess about half a mile away, all ATS.

We had an extra second subaltern ATS officer now. 'Aileen' and she and I became friends. A person named Carol Levis had arrived in the country from Canada looking for 'show biz' talent and I was invited to audition for him at Nottingham. Aileen went with me. It was quite a different experience and I passed his 'scrutiny' (I was at that time then known as a Carol Levis 'discovery').

Our ATS billet was in a sad state of disrepair so we were moved to a newer large house a few minutes away. This was much better. It meant a morning parade in the road outside (still very residential) and a morning march to the depot. I think we all enjoyed this.

At the beginning of August a United Concert was to be arranged by the units in and around Bristol in aid of the Lord Lieutenant's (Glosc.) Welfare Fund. I was asked to be the lead singer. We had a few rehearsals and the show took place in the Victoria Rooms, Bristol on the 14th and 15th August, 1944. I am able to be quite certain of this date as I still have the official printed programme, on which my name appears several times. We had the band of the North Staffordshire Regiment to accompany and the show was called "This Is It", presented before the Lord Lieutenant of Gloucestershire, all the officers in the area, troops, ATS and many important local people. It was a great success and I enjoyed myself thoroughly. The local paper took photos and I have one of these in my 'album' along with the programme.

Shortly after this I was invited to sing for the workers at an aircraft factory (north of Bristol). I had to obtain special permission to do this from my officer. This was given and I was also allowed transport; another enjoyable event.

Our troops in France were now covering much ground but a very sad event was the dropping of troops in Holland. It was a mistake; many were killed. One of the HQ officers had a brother who was dropped there and lost his life.

We were now having regular talks on Current Affairs and some instructive and educational evenings also.

Leave was back to normal and one bright ATS I had, passed me a 'fun' note (in my album) asked 'Dear Sgt' for a weekend pass. As sergeant in charge, all the applications for leave had to come to me first, before being passed to Coy Office. This was so that they did not overlap. Private Callaghan did of course rewrite her application!

But I am glad to say that keeping discipline and also a friendly touch was useful in our working unit and I had little trouble. I had to be 'Mother' as well as 'Sergeant' — a case follows. Our married couple still of course were in

In aid of the Lord Lieutenant's (Glos.) Welfare Fund

Units of Bristol Sub-District

PRESENT

"This is It"

The Army Entertains

WITH THE

Band of the
North Staffordshire Regiment

VICTORIA ROOMS, BRISTOL
Monday, August 14th, 1944
Tuesday, August 15th, 1944

PRICE 3d.

UNIFORM REHEARSAL FOR ARMY SHOW. Joint producers going over the script with members of the cast of "This is It," the Army show to be given at the Victoria Rooms next Monday and Tuesday.

Programme and newspaper cutting (author third front left)

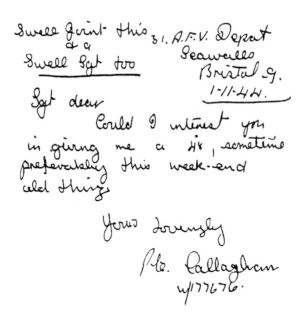

Joker Private Callaghan's application for leave.

separate billets until weekends off. The girl still in mine. She became pregnant and was hoping for release from ATS. At about 2.00 a.m. one morning I was awakened by knocks on my door. Half asleep I called "Come in." It was one of the girl's roommates.

She said "Dorothy is having a miscarriage."

I shot out of bed and pulled on trousers and top and dashed downstairs. I saw her and could not get quickly enough to a phone in Coy Office. We managed to raise help and an ambulance to get her to safety. I am afraid it upset us all, but she recovered well and was given leave.

I was called into Company Office one day and Miss Naish said that a Southern Command drill competition and display was shortly to take place at Taunton. Did I think our working unit was up to it? Of course I did and set to work on drill sessions with my girls. These had to take place in the road outside the billet (no such luxury as a barrack square) and we often had spectators which was good for the platoon to give them confidence.

They improved tremendously and were full of interest in the event and pleasure that they were able to take part; a day out!

The day arrived and a coach was duly booked to take us all to Taunton. I told the girls to travel in their second uniform and carry their no. 1 carefully pressed. Shoes and buttons were polished to a fine art.

We arrived and the girls (and myself) changed uniform in the coach. As there were thirty of them that day it was a bit of a tight fit, along with many giggles and 'That's my skirt!' etc., we got off the coach and they paraded. As it was late September it was a lovely fine day and not hot, so it was comfortable for drill. Our turn to 'show off' came and they were wonderful. No one put a foot wrong and I was very proud as I drilled them.

The results were, the next day, posted on Part 1 of Company Orders. I have the Coy Order. It states: *"All auxiliaries who took part in the Drill Competition at Taunton on Sep. 23rd are to be congratulated on obtaining 86% marks. This company obtained an 'Excellent' for the Instructor, Sgt. Crossley. The judges commented on the good shoes and buttons of the Company"*. They deserved it and we duly celebrated at the 'local'.

Christmas came and went, no leave for me, but the Christmas spirit was better than it had been for years.

Into another year and work at the Tank Depot continued on tanks and carriers — also one amphibian vehicle — which had been damaged, but of course caused great interest. All had to be repaired, cleaned and refitted.

I was still the only ATS sergeant but my life was neither lonely or solitary. More evenings were free and more time at weekends. I had invitations out from an Army sergeant who lived nearby to babysit for him and his wife so that they could have an evening out together. A new temporary Sandhurst officer — Captain Day invited me to tea with his wife. We had 'Ludo' competitions in the mess! (Paying

NOTICE S

DRILL COMPETITION.

All auxiliaries who took part in the Drill Competition at Taunton on Sep.23rd, are to be congratulated on obtaining 86% marks. This Company obtained an "Excellent" for the Instructor, Sgt. Crossley. The judges commented on the good shoes and butt ons of "F" Company.

CLOTHING.

The u/a auxiliaries will report to the Company Store at 18.00 hrs. on Friday, Sep.29th, for issue of the following:-

RUBBER BOOTS   —   Ptes Wyman, McHugh, Meier, Ough, Powell.

OVERALLS DENIM —   Ptes McHugh, Meier, Holt, Renshaw, Spedding, hite, Raynes.

JERKINS LEATHER —   Ptes O ugh, Meier, McHugh, Cooke, Elliott, Jones A, Powell, Renshaw, Gal l, Wyman, Holt, White, Gardner, Cooper C, Elliott.

Junior Commander
Commanding "B" Coy.,
Somerset & Bristol Group, A.T.S.

The results of the drill competition.

ha'penny per game!). Then came Captain Guscott's wedding — to which he invited eight representatives from the depot — myself included. Transport was arranged as it was in a village a few miles away from Bristol. We had a lovely day and wished him well — he was very well liked. I worked alongside a Staff Sergeant Selway (Army) and a few of us used to spend an occasional evening at a friend's house. She played a guitar, so we were able to have a singalong!

The inevitable company photo of us (ATS) had to be taken which I still have. I sat on the front row next to my officer Miss Naish with my girls and 'F' Coy ATS in rows behind us. It is a good photo.

On one of the pay parades about this time — Subaltern Naish stopped me and said, (jokingly) "I really do not enjoy paying you Sergeant Crossley — you get more money than I do!"

"Long service Ma'am and more courses!" I replied. We both laughed.

Captain Guscott took me on a day outing to Gloucester to a very large factory (where, I believe, matches used to be made) where now tanks were being made. An instructive and interesting day.

I sang at events in Bristol at this time — out of depot hours — and was quite often given a cash gift as a thank you. After all, I did have to get there and also buy new song sheets occasionally.

May 1945 arrived and I received (via my OC) a request to ask if I would sing in Bristol Cathedral. This was to be a service of Thanksgiving for the end of hostilities in Europe. I was honoured to be asked to sing there.

On May 17th I presented myself at the cathedral and was shown to the forefront seat of the choir stalls. There were 1,000 people in the congregation, and I sang as requested, 'Jerusalem'. The acoustics were wonderful — the organist played just right and I really enjoyed singing. A few days later I received a 'Thank you' letter and an Active Service Edition Bible from Miss Morris the organiser. I still have both letter and prayer book — inscribed.

The company photograph — author seated eighth from right.

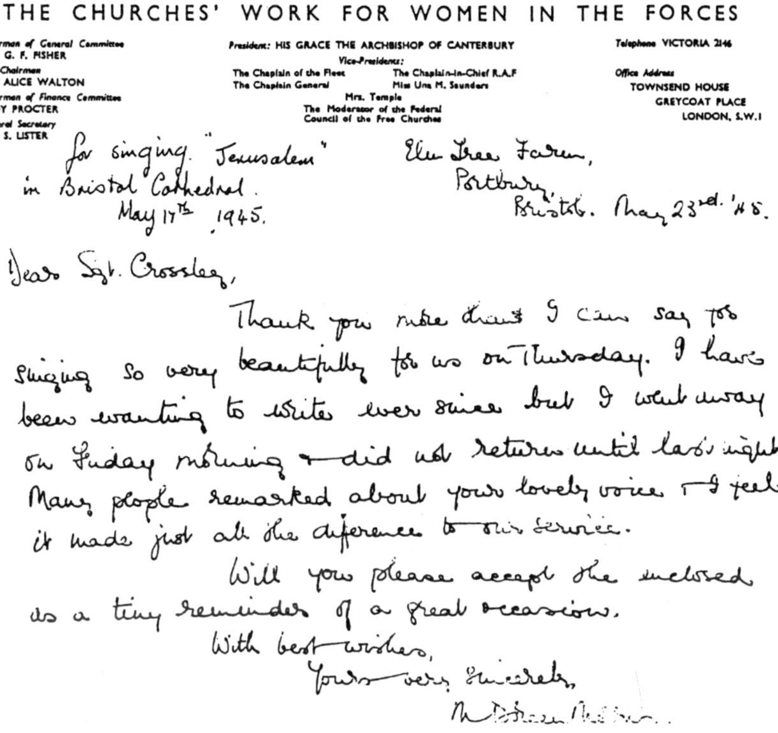
THE CHURCHES' WORK FOR WOMEN IN THE FORCES

Chairman of General Committee Mrs. G. F. FISHER
Vice-Chairman Miss ALICE WALTON
Chairman of Finance Committee LADY PROCTER
General Secretary Miss S. LISTER

President: HIS GRACE THE ARCHBISHOP OF CANTERBURY
Vice-Presidents:
The Chaplain of the Fleet
The Chaplain-in-Chief R.A.F.
The Chaplain General
Miss Una M. Saunders
Mrs. Temple
The Moderator of the Federal Council of the Free Churches

Telephone VICTORIA 2146
Office Address TOWNSEND HOUSE GREYCOAT PLACE LONDON, S.W.1

for singing "Jerusalem"
in Bristol Cathedral.
May 17th 1945.

Elm Tree Farm,
Portbury,
Bristol. May 23rd. '45.

Dear Sgt. Crossley,

Thank you more than I can say for singing so very beautifully for us on Thursday. I have been wanting to write ever since but I went away on Friday morning & did not return until last night. Many people remarked about your lovely voice & I feel it made just all the difference to our service.

Will you please accept the enclosed as a tiny reminder of a great occasion.

With best wishes,
Yours very sincerely,
[illegible]

A letter received after singing in Bristol Cathedral.

After this more invitations to sing in Bristol arrived, but at this time I had quite a lot of duties and could not take up many invitations.

I did take up an audition at the BBC Centre, Whiteladies Road, Bristol. It was interesting to see what happened and I must admit to a slight feeling of 'nerves'. Nevertheless it must have been quite good as later in the Autumn I received an offer from a newly formed Entertainments Company called "Stars in Battledress" which I was invited to join upon my demobilisation from the Army. Some will probably remember a TV star 'Ted Ray' musician and comedian who was then a new member of the company ('Ray's a laugh' as he was then known).

CHAPTER 9

Demob

I was now coming up to my twenty-fifth birthday, and demob was looming on the horizon. Some of the older girls and married ones had now gone.

Two days per week we were given cookery lessons at a school about a mile away. Someone must have wakened up to the fact that many of us had had all our cooking done for us for five years or more, and probably could not even boil an egg successfully. They were great fun and brightened up our lives considerably. In the mornings we jointly (about eight of us each day) made our communal dinner and in the afternoons made cakes, which we were able to bring back to the billet and share (if edible!).

A ship had docked at Bristol carrying many New Zealand sailors and some were invited up to the Tank Depot to see what kind of work the ATS had been doing. One charmer — Jack Bell, held me in conversation for some time — he wanted to talk about his family in Waikato, North Island, NZ. I think he was homesick.

I had my first and only ride on the back of a motorbike at about this time. One of the sergeants invited me to go to the 'Dogs' (greyhound race track) with him. Both ride and visit were an education which I have never repeated! I felt safer on a tank!

A few years ago I visited an Army Training Unit in Lancashire. The men had *duvets* on their beds, bedside tables with photos, etc. Radios, televisions, stereos, mobile phones?

How did we manage to keep ourselves occupied without all these luxuries?

Demob drew nearer. I was torn three ways. My mother was asking me to go home. She was not well at this time and had many worries with four of us being away from home throughout the war. My three brothers had all now married and were to return to their own homes. Mother was sending me advertisements of local jobs — to tempt me I think. Jobs were to be hard to come by for quite some time. The 'Stars in Battledress' had sent me another letter urging me to make a decision to join them. Lastly and certainly not least — I could sign up in the Army for a further three years.

Considering the 'Stars in Battledress' — I felt that at twenty-five years old it was a bit risky to give up all for that when I might not last very long in 'show biz'. There must be younger ones coming along. I longed to remain in the Army, it seemed to have become my life and as a sergeant life was good. My mother drew my conscience and I decided to take demob. I must say at this point, that I was unhappy for many weeks on returning home and almost signed-up again. But after all, the job for which I had joined the ATS had been done successfully, and it was time to move on.

I was given a date early in January 1946 so I arranged an evening out at the theatre in Bristol for many of my friends. The show included solos sung by Betty Driver a lovely young woman with a good voice. She is now known as 'Betty' — the barmaid in Coronation Street. In the same show was Cyril Fletcher — I believe he was then, her husband. We had a good and enjoyable evening out — meeting up with the rest of my platoon at the 'local'. It would give me great joy to meet any of those wonderful ATS again, from 31st AFV.

Two days later it was farewell to the ATS. I was demobbed on the 6th January 1946. Strangely this was the day my future husband (whom I had yet to meet) was also demobbed from the RAF. To complete the circle my son David was born on 6th January three years later. I was demobbed where I first started out — at Fulford Barracks,

York. It brought back many memories, as writing this account has done.

If I brought any joy by my singing, as a reprieve from war worries, to any of the troops throughout the war, I can only be thankful that I was able to do so. I enjoyed having the opportunities to sing.

I am proud to have been part of World War II in the Auxiliary Territorial Service (ATS). I had given five years of my young life to my country in time of need — willingly and without regret. My medals are worn with pride on Armistice Day each year.

My demob gratuity for war service was £48.15 shillings. My demob book reads: CONDUCT — EXEMPLARY.

MESSAGE FROM CHIEF CONTROLLER, L. E. WHATELEY, C.B.E., DIRECTOR AUXILIARY TERRITORIAL SERVICE, TO ALL RANKS A.T.S. ON RELEASE

Your task with the Army is completed. In the name of the Auxiliary Territorial Service I thank you. You have served your King and Country in such a way as to uphold the highest traditions of British womanhood.

I have, therefore, no hesitation in reminding you that, to secure a Lasting Peace, we must one and all continue not only to make sacrifices but a definite contribution, according to our circumstances, to our Country.

You have already proved that you know the true meaning of Service, " An act performed for the benefit of a cause and not necessarily to the benefit of an individual."

Let us then pledge ourselves to be true to those who have given their lives, that their sacrifice may not be in vain.

Good luck and God speed.

L. P. Whateley

RELEASE LEAV

Army No. *W/ 89104.*   Present Rank *WS/SC*

Surname (Block Letters) *CROSSLEY.*

Christian Name/s *ELSIE MAY.*

Coy. and Group/Unit *3. COY. GLOS. 8/0. GPO.*

Da   *Calling-up inapplicable.

(a)   (c) Se

(b) *..*   (d) An

CLASSES. III. II. I.

Military Conduct :

EXEM OLARY.

Testimonial: *SGT. CROSSLEY HAS HELD A AND RESPONSIBILITY WHICH SHE HAS C COMPLETE SATISFACTION. ABLE TO CON SMART AND ALERT MANNER. PUNC*

Place *BRISTOL.*   Date ....

Demobilisation documents.

A List of Some of the Songs I Sang During the War

Not Understood
Love is My Reason
We'll Gather Lilacs
My Heart and I
The World is Mine
I Love Thee (Grieg)
Dream O' Day Jill
In an Old Fashioned Town
Land of Hope and Glory
Someday We Shall Meet Again
Waltz of My Heart
I'll Follow My Secret Heart
Because / and — So Deep is the Night
Bird Songs at Eventide
Song of Liberty
Can I Forget You
I'll See You Again
Sing Joyous Bird
When You Come Home
Jerusalem
Solveigs Song
Ave Maria
Shine Through My Dreams